Cloud Dance

THOMAS LOCKER

HARCOURT, INC.

Orlando   Austin   New York   San Diego   Toronto   London

Manufactured in China

CLOUDS OF MANY shapes
and sizes drift and dance across
the sky.

In every time and season
the colors of clouds
are always changing.

Brilliant sunset clouds
glow
and then fade.

Nighttime clouds
with silver edges
shimmer in the moonlight.

High, wispy clouds
race
in the autumn wind.

Winter clouds,
low and thick,
bring sparkling snow.

Soft, rosy spring clouds
flow
in the dawn light.

Veils of mist

rise

in warm sunlight.

Delicate morning clouds
grow
and form.

Fluffy summer clouds
march
in the blue sky.

Gray clouds
with golden fringes
block the streaming sunlight.

Dark-and-light
storm clouds
tower.

Rain clouds,
full and heavy,
burst.

Water rising,
forming clouds of many
shapes and colors
that drift and dance
across the sky.
Good-night clouds.

ABOUT CLOUDS

How high does the sky reach?

The envelope of gases surrounding the earth is composed of water vapor and gases, including nitrogen, oxygen, carbon dioxide, and tiny amounts of other gases. This envelope of gases and water vapor is called the atmosphere, and it extends upward from the surface of the earth for more than three hundred miles. The layer nearest the earth is called the troposphere. It is where clouds form and where our weather occurs. This layer extends upward for five to ten miles. It is thickest above the Tropics, and reaches its thinnest points over the polar regions.

How are clouds formed?

When the warmth and energy of sunlight act upon water in lakes, streams, oceans, or even mud puddles, the water becomes water vapor. This vapor attaches to microscopic dust particles released into the atmosphere by volcanic eruptions and smoke, particles from outer space, and salt particles released through the crashing of waves. The dust and water vapor rise and are cooled as the atmosphere cools. Eventually the temperature drops far enough, and the water vapor is returned to its liquid state. Millions and millions of these water droplets and dust particles combined make a cloud.

How many kinds of clouds are there?

Observers have categorized clouds in two ways: altitude and appearance. There are four classes of clouds based on altitude:

1. high
2. midlevel
3. low
4. clouds that extend upward through more than one level

Within each of these altitude categories, different cloud shapes are visible. (See the chart on the facing page.) **Cirrus clouds** usually occur at high altitudes and often look like wispy hair. **Cumulus clouds** are white and fluffy, like big piles of cotton balls, and are mostly found at low altitudes. Most **stratus clouds** form at lower elevations. These thick blankets can cover the entire sky.

Combinations of these basic shapes are also common. For example, **cirrocumulus clouds** are high-level clouds that are long and wispy, yet thicker and rounder than a basic cirrus cloud.

It takes practice to recognize and name clouds. Clouds are in a constant state of change and appear in an infinite variety of shapes. Some clouds do not fit neatly into basic categories. For instance, unicus clouds are like commas resting on their sides. Fractus clouds, with ragged edges, are really pieces of broken clouds. And, of course, clouds can drift and float from one elevation to another.

Why are clouds different colors?

Cloud observers do not use color as a way to classify clouds. This is because the color of clouds comes from sunlight. At midday, when the sun is directly overhead, the sky appears blue and the clouds white. In the early morning or at sunset, when the sun is low on the horizon and further away, the slanting sun rays make the clouds appear in beautiful shades of rose, purple, gold, and orange. All sky colors are a result of the interplay of light, water vapor, and dust particles in the air.

Scientific information was researched and written by Candace Christiansen, who is the author of several books for children and has taught science for more than ten years.

TYPES OF CLOUDS

Cirrostratus: high-level sheetlike clouds
(above 18,000 feet)

Cirrus: high-level wispy clouds
(above 18,000 feet)

Cirrocumulus: high-level thin, patchy clouds
(above 18,000 feet)

Altostratus: middle-level sheetlike clouds
(6,000 to 20,000 feet)

Cumulonimbus: high-level towering clouds
(ground level to 50,000 feet)

Altocumulus: middle-level patchy clouds
(6,000 to 20,000 feet)

Stratocumulus: low-level sheets of puffy clouds
(below 6,000 feet)

Cumulus: low-level puffy clouds
(below 6,000 feet)

Stratus: low-level flat clouds
(below 6,000 feet)

To my sister, Barbara
—T. L.

www.HarcourtBooks.com

Library of Congress Cataloging-in-Publication Data
Locker, Thomas, 1937–
Cloud dance/by Thomas Locker.
p.   cm.
Summary: Clouds of many shapes and sizes drift and dance across
the sky. Includes factual information on the formation and different
kinds of clouds.
[1. Clouds — Fiction.]   I. Title.
PZ7.L7945Cl   2000
[E]–dc21   99-42642
ISBN-13: 978-0-15-202231-0
ISBN-10: 0-15-202231-7

G I K M N L J H F

The illustrations in this book were done in oils on canvas.
The display calligraphy was hand lettered by John Stevens.
The display type was set in Engravers Roman.
The text type was set in Berkeley Old Style.
Printed by South China Printing Company, Ltd., China
This book was printed on totally chlorine-free
Grycksbo Matte paper.
Production supervision by Ginger Boyer
Designed by Ivan Holmes